What touches Mallika Bhaumik's poetry is the personal touch to a variety of topics in a fractured and dissolving world. There is the blending of objectivity and subjectivity, an amalgamation of psychic time with history-personal and otherwise. Time as a layered entity with both past and present freezes and sometimes disappears to become a solid ground for the mind to traverse. Inanimate things like stones get expanded into a poetic landscape. The poems are a dance towards and away from poetic limitation, sometimes they falter and at other times the sensual, metaphysical are fused in this movement.

Sharmila Ray

How Not To Remember

Mallika Bhaumik

HAWAKAL

HAWAKAL

Published by Hawakal Publishers
185 Kali Temple Road, Nimta, Kolkata 700049
India

Email info@hawakal.com
Website www.hawakal.com

First edition November, 2019

Cover art: shutterstock
Cover design: Bitan Chakraborty

ISBN: 978-93-87883 90-1

Price: INR 300 | USD 11.99

To
my sons,
Rishabh and *Ritwik*

Overruling Impermanence

Marcel Proust starts his novel *Remembrance of Things Past* (also in literal translation of French called *In Search of Lost Time*) with the words "For a long time I used to go to bed early" expressing his anxiety of leaving his mother at night. The novel is about memory and how through art lost time can be reclaimed at least in the mind. Proust had a deep sense of the loss of loved ones as well as the loss of affection itself. That is why the opening lines display a kind of separation anxiety and the last book of the mammoth seven volume novel is titled "Time Regained." The novel often uses the technique of flashback to explore the protagonist's nostalgia and transform it into art in order to preserve it in the mind. Mallika Bhaumik in her second volume of poetry does the same thing of transforming nostalgia into products of art. Ironically, her second book of poems is titled *How Not to Remember*, perhaps because once remembrance is transformed into art it need not be recalled as it does not remain transient. Once lost time is regained through the words of a poem it attains permanence.

In the title poem Mallika Bhaumik writes "let the minutes and seconds run amok and merge themselves into timelessness" and concludes the poem with the lines:

As you feel light and weightless; the burden of memory eases off,
you are done with your name;
now mingle with the thin air around and become the grey dusk .

This is how memory is made timeless and nostalgia becomes a product of art. In the poem titled "Remembrance" she writes: "in fact, we are all forgotten somewhere/ in time/ like the long dark shadows of night/ are forgotten/ by sunbathed verandahs." It is this duel between remembering and forgetting which gives birth to anxiety and for a poet it is this anxiety that gives birth to words. Mallika Bhaumik knows how to transform nostalgia into art by the usage of words in poems. She can make the night swim "in the pool of her eyes," she can read "undeciphered sorrow," she can make solitude fall in drops, she can make silence scatter and fall apart, she can transform love into a lone goldfish, she can understand the syllables of rain even if they are in a different dialect, she can unbury the fossils of alphabets, she can make loss germinate, she can read the nights which are essays in loneliness, she can heap loss and forget the story she lives in. It is this uncanny ability to raise the words from the level of communication to the level of art that makes Mallika Bhaumik a poet.

In her poem titled "Colours" Mallika Bhaumik writes, "between our words and worlds life froze." The poet freezes life into art by finding lost time and embalming it. It is a necessity because time is constantly getting wiped out from memory and like Proust this deep sense of loss makes the poet uneasy and brings in anxiety. There is tension between wanting stasis and the perpetual dynamics of elision, erosion, weathering, and forgetting. She says in the poem "Rainwashed":

A river flows through us
as we talk,
our words float
carrying the moments we did not talk about.

In fact she almost echoes the title of Proust's novel when she says in the poem "Some Other Nights": "I search for time."

Time that will not stay and can only be captured by what Keats called "negative capability," time that is composed of rain-sodden memories, time that is like the muddy water of remembrance, time that is like the fading line of evening, time that is what is Mallika Bhaumik's preoccupation. In the poem "Annihilation" she asks, "Is this the place where the world ends?" and leaves the reader to answer it and arrest the question from sliding and falling. This is a fine collection which itself will arrest readers and in that moment of reading the readers will become one with the art, an art that negates impermanence.

Amit Shankar Saha
November 8, 2019
Calcutta

Acknowledgements

I would start my acknowledgement by expressing my gratitude to *Hawakal Publishers* for having faith in my work and creating a beautiful home for my poems in the shape of this poetry book.

I would also take this opportunity to thank the editors of the following magazines and anthologies for being the first publisher of many of my poems, like *Cafe Dissensus, Narrow Road, The Wagon Magazine, Oddball Magazine, Glomag, Get Bengal, Duane's Poetree, Shot Glass Journal, In Parentheses* journal, *Mark Literary Review, Spark Magazine, The Pangolin Review, The Metaworker, Mad Swirl, The Local Train Magazine, The Woman Inc, Harbringer Asylum, Equiverse Space Anthology, Muffled Moans Anthology*, and I would also like to thank the editors of the upcoming anthology, *Artery* by Kritya poetry movement, and Walking BookFairs for accepting my work.

My poetic journey would not have started at all if I had not received constant support and encouragement from a few fellow poets, readers, and mentors who have constantly read and encouraged me. In this regard I would like to mention *Amit Shankar Saha* (he has also written the foreword for this book), *Jagari Mukherjee, Lopa Banarjee, Sudeshna Mukherjee, Vijay Nair, Smeetha Bhowmik, Vivek Periera, Ashok kumar Mitra* and fellow poet and brother, *Ronald Tuhin D'Rozario*.

I would also extend my thanks to *Ampat Koshy* and *Santosh Bakaya* for their support.

I am grateful to *Sharmila Ray* for the beautiful blurb that she has penned for this book .

I sincerely thank my friends, close relatives, old acquaintances who have wished me well during this journey.

My vocabulary fails me when it comes to thanking people who are closest to me. My family is my greatest strength and I thank my parents, my husband, *Rahul*, and my sons, *Rishabh* and *Ritwik*, for being in my life and for giving it meaning and direction.

Contents

The Third Eye

Night swims in the pool
of her eyes
the lover that never was,
spreads himself,
the dusk of her skin,
the doe eyes,
those that prompted the poet to call her
'krishnakali',
look up to see the circling blades
the jingling bangles count the moments.
The melancholy of *Bhairavi* trails off
–'my armlets are falling off'
the dreams of beloved's home
hide behind a cracked mirror.
Memories of hopscotch days
run along the kaash field,
the whistle of the train beckons.

Durga sits on a tulip painted bedsheet,
clutching a crisp pink note
The blooming buds of mogras
twisted around her plait,
lie scattered.
Her window opens to a dingy lane
of worn out tales,
the eyes do not see a sky,
the embers of the night's rage
faintly colour the distant horizon,
–the third eye.

Unaccounted

There is a lost language
for some undeciphered sorrow
they are like small changes
unaccounted for,
often lying like the last swig remaining
at the bottom of the glass
as we move on to mourn other losses,
a death, a diagnosis or a betrayal.

Purple is their colour,
unwept memories of some lost trinket,
some unanswered call
missing marbles of childhood,
or selling away of grandfather's favourite gramophone,
poetry of Agha Shahid Ali
on windswept monsoon nights.

I have some such stories forming
an archipelago in my heart
they do not dissolve like the sunset hues
they have no closures at all,
and it is for them that every year
I fall in love with the colours of the fall.

Conversation

Acceptance is the best way
they say,
so I let go the questions,
they slide,
they fall,
like burnt out crackers losing their gunpowder;
a torn sky looks on.
Our sharpness rounded off
we too decide to carry on,
amicably.

You and I sit down with coffee,
we talk of the regular things–
rising price, calorie counts, colleagues
and relatives
I tell you, "it's better to cook in olive oil,"
and we munch on the cookies.
Some irksome shadows lurk around
the fringes of our words,
our faces become the walls of our old home
colours peeling off,
why is it that I feel your furtive glances
around the room?
I stir the spoon
dissolving myself in the aromatic brew.
The scum of my soul surfaces,
I shudder to see
–a chameleon!

Tales of Solitude

I hear solitude falling in drops,
the empty bucket gets filled up.
A drop,
a pause,
and another,
the silence of the house punctuated
at regular intervals.
I keep counting till I lose count,
numerous feelings float
in the translucence of the eyes
and I chase the days
the washed away sandcastles,
the brine of the sea bringing in distant memories,
the ones I wish to touch; the ones I wish away.

The street lights,
their dim glow casting dim shadows
of long lost lullabies,
some left behind
in time's forgotten alleys
while some, on a lonely November night,
leak out of my abscessed heart
in tiny droplets.

Water Colour

The haunting tune
of monsoon,
an old craving sprouts from beneath the mulch
and my rain sodden memories
like dense ponderous clouds
of a far away land
inch closer and closer,
then burst and collapse.
I breathe in the moisture of the air.

I look out,
see the intriguing wet darkness,
my desolate lane
the blurred light of the street lamp
and the sharp arrows of rain creating a water colour,
beautiful yet plaintive.

A face is overlapped by another
and yet another...
and all these faces are mine,
brush strokes of unspoken words,
the smudged hues of their pain
painting the contours
of my desires,
and erasing them
again.

Reclamation

Someday we might meet,
when time has melted in us,
our lives look like dried river beds
Would you then recognise my face?

My face might appear unknown,
remote like the rugged terrains of Tibet
with its etched contours of pain,
patient as wisdom, mysterious
as some ancient knowledge.
Would it be the same face
you sought through long lonely nights?
The melancholy strain of some
ancient lore mingling with
shifting dunes of sands.
Your mouth gone dry, a sea churning within.
A lost kiss.

Would it still be so dear that
you would travel through
the ruins of rebirth to call me again?

The earth has saved the receding sound waves,
fossils of the alphabets of my name.

Apology

Some words just refuse to be born,
they lie like cinders of the cold hearth,
clouds of our burnt feelings
grieving grey,
the walls sweat out claustrophobia.

I too drift away; shedding my old skin,
my indifference growing,
and the worn out feel,
brittle yellow pages of the address book;
we no longer need.
Yet we let our fatigued bodies
believe we have each other,
slowly I blend into the blue of the night
and you cannot reach.
The silence; dark and wary,
quietly covers us

Our promises are like cut out kites,
by the verandah our potted greens die,
I weep for them,
my teardrops ink an apology.

Nurtured

There is a distance that waits between you and me,
our bed; a rift valley between two sleeping landmasses,
between being close and getting estranged,
between screaming scars and numb silence.
Someday... far away in time,
we, two weary incomplete poems;
the grey of dusk smeared on our faces
sit on a park bench
among browning leaves.

The slipped away moments keep tugging us,
we gather and string them in
a pattern that speaks of nurturing;
creating wholeness out of fragments
in a city of short lived happiness.

The City My Muse

A love that unreasonably
stretches between the cantilevers
of a bridge, joining its twin city
over a muddy river
at the fag end of her journey.
A love that has flipped the archived pages
of history of defiance,
old serpentine lanes breathing the tales of Swadeshi.
A love that runs barefoot to the ghat
where the the symbol of Nari Shakti,
Durga is immersed,
and the rambunctious kids play in the mud
cheering for her next year's arrival.

The fluid emotions of the soccer fields,
a sip of chai from the steaming earthen mugs,
the hot kathi rolls and rosogollas of K C Das,
the gleam in the eyes during monsoon,
when silvery hilsas throng the bazaar.
That's my city ,that has seen me
blossoming into a woman.

I have also seen her in her gentler mood at night,
singing to me a lullaby
as the last tram hums by
making me fall hopelessly in love
with its vigilant neon lights,
dogs and people often curling up
at the quiet corners of the streets.

Bird Cries
song of protest

A morning comes wrapped in silence
in this walled city,
its bridges and parks, museums, eateries,
clock tower wear a solemn look
the breeze too blows with caution,
it feels no flutter around it.
We look at each other
trying to gauge what is amiss.
A whisper goes around,
"where have the birds gone?"

An old fakir sits by the bazaar gate
his ektara hums another tune; a tune of bird protest.
How songs of freedom
have been quashed and throttled, how?
people have been cloaked in green or saffron or red,
how they have flown away leaving behind the corn,
how we are left to wonder,
where have the birds gone?

People of this land have lost their tongues
they speak nothing, they speak to none,
different bird cries fill the empty spaces of their mind.
They toddle around long after the birds have gone.

Old Neighbours

The nights grow dense,
the weary shadows of the day
merge themselves with the darkness,
–a darkness that remains mute witness
to the spilled dreams on the sidewalk,
–dogs and humans co habit
their territories clearly marked.
All shrivelled up,
bundled,
yet
breathing,
breeding,
weaving the fabric
of their insignificant lives.
Some nights go deep inside their bones
some nights pause before the final bite,
some nights crawl in silently to script
the epilogue of their unfairy lives.

The vacant corners are again occupied.
Some other migrant arms
sell newspapers, rose bunches, agarbattis
at traffic snarls
some other wintry nights claim them perhaps.
The city folds its paper heart,
only the dogs at times,
sniff and look around for their old neighbours

Refugee

Ah! if life could only script a different tale!
The soil bearing the imprint of their foot
marks not foreign.
The windblown dandelions
carrying the fragrance of their land,
The timeless arch of the sky spread above;
clouds floating freely
No walls, no wires, no gun toting military,
But their eyes see an altered world,
Where tomorrow hangs precariously
Their feet tread over an alien earth,
unwelcome,
Being hurled out of home,
crossing the border with lesser human identities,
Refugees.

(This is a reverse poem, it can also be read from bottom to top.)

A Fallen Durga

Kumartuli is abuzz with noise,
it's the auspicious month of *Ashwin*,
a fallen woman's trodden earth
is used for bringing a warrior woman to life,
to be awed, revered, worshipped.
Her arms, limbs, eyes,
the pink pouty lips under the neon lights,
the stained bedsheet
witness to the ravenous nights.
Silhoutted demons
nibbling at her curves and mounds
as the goddess ebbs away
merging into the nude darkness of bamboo and hay.
The skeletal remains of a hushed story
drowned under maddening dhak beats,
while the lotus,the shiuli, the kaash
bloom under a different sky.

Blindness

A screeching halt,
a stretch of a busy highway,
limbs tossed in the air,
the white SUV swerves
and speeds off.

Faith floating in eyes
dry fruits and pashmina,
folded hands, bejewelled fingers.
Any astral stone, any *tabeez*
to tame the uncertainties of life?

A room half lit, spartan,
an ascetic's dreamy gaze
looks on, looks within, looks beyond,
a potion comes,
–a cure for blindness.

Unborn

The swirling blackhole nearing,
a harsh cold pierces the pink of my flesh
the blood vessels dilate; about to burst
the rhythm of my mom's body,
the warmth of her womb's fluid love, sadly missing.
I, an unwanted unborn breath,
plucked and thrown out before budding,
keep shivering; gasping for breath.

My mother doesnot weep for me,
her hands assure the warmth of her sons'
bodies under the *rajai*; she pulls over,
they sleep comfortably,
I, a nameless embryo; a vessel of life,
shrink and diminish to become a speck,
slowly merge into nihility.

Homecoming

His heart hides a sky
his eyes long to see,
the coagulated blood vessels
swell, as his wishes travel
over the barbed wire,
where the syllable of rain
has a different dialect.
As his limbs gradually stiffen,
a pair of truant feet of long ago,
run along the aisle of the harvested fields
and a lung full of inhaled air
breathes out o'er an inch of earth
where the dampened smell of 'home' nestles,
without the legitimacy
of a ration card.

Cityscape

The city swallows time
the vices of men are washed and
hung out to dry on square terraces.
The nook of the ninth storey balcony;
a bird's eye view,
the roving lens and a chaotic labyrinthine spread.
an indifferent city, chewing the cud;
living the old tale,
and it is here,
that he picks up the shards of his early days.

Each click is a patchwork of emotions
a loss woven in simmering rage,
a conflict or a futile search.
A rare click of a mother bird tending
her nestlings through the canopy of green
churns the memory of an elderly child,
till it spills over a leaking tiled roof.

His young mother's shriek, her legs pulled apart,
some moving shadows
some burnt chapatis,
–a lost childhood.

Rainwashed

A river flows through us
as we talk,
our words float
carrying the moments we did not talk about.
They move towards an end; blurred and hazy
they speak of a nascent sorrow,
greying.

The present sits numb
with tall mugs of coffee,
and then plunges into the disorder of
wordlessness.

The bustling street and the hawkers' voice,
I walk past an array of colourful wares
along the Gariahat stretch.
It has rained a while ago,
the city looks nubile, soft, wet
like a woman just after bath.
Somewhere... a loss germinates.

It's just five and there's an eternity to live.
The colours spill.

Keepsake

A journey starts,
chugging towards a foggy distance.
A damp routine waits.
A pain, dry and numb, sits snugly within.
I turn the pages of a magazine.

A journey is coming near or going far.
Some crocheted memories, photographs,
handwritten letters.
A lost door, its peeping keyhole,
a childhood fading with the rush of the suburbs,
some yesterday's broken pieces glued to today's tale.
A redundant key.
I carry them as keepsakes.
My mother's zari bordered peach saree,
her favourite pearl bracelet.

*Chaiwallah*s and noise of other hawkers
selling chewing gums, combs, cheap nail cutters.
My fingers reach an asylum of touch,
the lusty pearls ,the softness of the peach drape.
There are no lavenders blooming,
I inhale her lavender fragrance.

Defiance

A tapestry of woven words covers her,
the moss laden bricks of her old house,
roots of aswath (peepal) forcing their way through,
she too, has outgrown her years.

The toothless gum smiles,
she has seen death, betrayal, vice,
her blood drained away prematurely
during the Naxalbari days,
the empty rooms echo the footsteps of time,
her eyes fail to see through the cobweb of memories.

Yet, she wears red,
yet she is defiant,
her every breath is a reminder,
she is another *Hajar churashi r maa*(Mother of 1084).

Inspired by '*Hajar Churashir Maa*' , a novel by Mahasweta
Devi, on the Naxal movement (a mother whose son's corpse
number was 1084 in the morgue)

Moneyplant

A glass jar; fat bellied; stands by her windowside;
bottling in some sunshine.
It remains neck filled with water
tender wishes of a money plant come out of it.
They are just like hers, shy, green, velvety,
talking in silent syllables.
One night she senses them taking a flight,
the curled up sighs opening like petals
their fragrance spreading o'er the unworded letters,
a heap of loss.
She forgets the story she lives in
floats like the roots of the moneyplant

The air grows thinner and thinner, drawing patterns,
the room and the window grow minuscule
as darkness carries her,
only the jade hearts of the leaves glow.

Wren

Days are just printed digits
on the calendar,
rows of mundanity
moving heavily; a goods train
I travel across the length of my mind
to stop at a time;
when I lip silent prayers
in a dim lit room
the pain of life beeping in a monitor
and the tiptoeing of an unnamed moment
putting the graph to rest,
while the call of azaan flows.

A loss gradually becomes unused stuff kept in the attic,
gathers dust
and loneliness becomes familiar.
I gain weight and blood pressure
and some helpful friends,
I also work for underprivileged children;
it lifts and cheers my heart,
where; in some obscure corner
a sorrow nestles,
tiny as a wren.

Some Other Nights

Nights are essays in loneliness
words scrawled in the dark
none to be retrieved,
I stretch on the bed; disheveled like my hair,
twinning with the night.
My flesh sinks
far below, a famished city blinks.
Nights have lost their chastity.
they stand stark naked, tired breasts sigh,
they have no mysteries to guard
they weave no dreams for lovers.

I search for time-fleeting, disloyal,
a longing for the things that
once drew the graffiti of my life.
They slowly fade like plaintive rays of the sinking sun.
A slice of a room,
an earthen pitcher,
the overweight sling bag,
stacks of reading materials
and star dotted nights spread outside
the window bars.

Colours

Colours deepened in my eyes
the blue of midnight memories
splayed all over,
windblown dandelions of another time.

The lazy tram rides on summer noons by the Maidan
walks across Boi Para,
the woody dusty smell of old books,
and infinite dreams tingling like
small changes in our pockets,
life looked vibrant like clusters of the blazing palash;
its unbridled passion
rubbed off on us.

The bubbles of the summer days
became the words of our poetry,
and somewhere
between our words and our worlds,
life froze
–a still shot in monochrome

palaash– flame of the forest (flower)
Boi para– College Street area of kolkata where there are
        rows of book shops selling books.
Maidan– a vast open green in Kolkata

Distance

As I walk,
this balmy Kolkata evening makes me
look at the the elongated shadow
of my memory
falling on the asphalt,
losing itself
in the brightening white of the neon.
I don't see you or myself
I don't reach anywhere; to any place.
There is only a sense of distance,
distance; that your lips had once trodden
on the geography of my skin,
distance; that might show me as a disappearing speck,
a melancholy canvas; some blotted out hues,
the dusky skyline of the city; an old sentinel,
slim branches of krishnachuras spreading their rage
and a shadow that walks on.
The seasons change.

The summers, springs and autumns,
have become a stilled breath
and all the touch,
smell and sound that remotely resemble you,
remain coiled in me as distance.

krishnachura– royal ponicia or gulmohor

Stone

I read time's calligraphy on your body
that has gulped the sun, wind, rain
you have years of silence within you
ancient grains of pain.
I see deep deep inside of you
and touch the dense stillness there,
it's like touching my own old wounds
in concentric circles of a felled tree trunk.
There's a wait in you
there's a wait in me
a knot of eternity stuck in the breast.
Am I a stone like you?
Do you have a heart like me? A bolted door?
The words dissolve in the quietude
It's only you and me and the curvature of the night,
we smear our darkness on each other.

Annihilation

The silence of the cold hills
scatters and falls apart;
a strange bird cry– shrill, sharp,
stabs the air.
An absence takes a plunge; steep as a canyon
I stand by the window; watch myself,
a falling snowflake
losing my shape, disintegrating,
my hands, limbs not with me,
the heart flung off
somewhere in the past.
I travel nevertheless,
the masked face lands noiselessly, I wonder,
"Is this the place where the world ends?"

There are no marks on the snow
There is nothing of me.

How Not To Remember

Let the afternoon melt and spread all over,
so much so that the it ceases to be.

Let the date swirl back to being nothing;
let the minutes and seconds run amok
and merge themselves into timelessness.

Let it all go, the moments cupped
and held with so much love
watch them burn in the palm and merge
with the lightness of the afternoon sun.

Let the whiteness of the walls dilate
and blur the pupils of the eye
still like an adamant ultraviolet ray
your lover's face might flash again.

Go out take a walk,
parks and cafes used to be your favourite haunts.

Let each touch ebb away as your feet
caress the green of the grass,
allow your body to float like bubbles in the park;
a young girl puffs out and then tries to catch

As you feel light and weightless;
the burden of memory eases off,
you are done with your name;
now mingle with the thin air around
and become the grey dusk.

Door

The darkness of the night is a ballerina,
my eyes are shut
while wishes widen to become
the span of an eagle's spread out wings,
and between feathery sleep and wakefulness,
I see a door,
crumbling brick walls around it
and one can see what's behind,
yet the door, like a stern guard
stands with a rusty lock.

Where is such a door... I wonder,
in some nameless street of childhood
or lost in the mist of folklores grandma used to narrate?
in some old rambling fort or ruins of a palace
I visited as an eager student of history,
or perhaps,
inside the deep dark well of an unresolved fear,
a door; that becomes my body
carrying scribblings of sad exiled dreams on its skin,
jaded,pale yellowish with riverine veins,
and if one presses an ear, one gets to hear
ripples of anguish,
songs of resilience.

Confession

A summer noon waits in my eyes
its hibiscus rage
simmering,
till the sultriness of this city scatters,
the mad rush of Kalbaisakhi,
bringing back the days
left lying in the attic of time.

They are like confessions of a fugitive
seeping into each membrane
spreading all over,
becoming me,
I smell like the damp walls of home
tenderness wrapped.
Belongingness is another human need.

Somewhere,
shadows of pain are like fronds of a palm tree
I leave them grieving,
my skin drinks the song of rain
an endless song; rippling,
some paper boats float ferrying
bubbles of happiness.

kalboisakhi–local storm accompanied by thunder showers
in Bengal during April . It is also called Nor'westers

Betrayal

On some heady *shravan* night like this,
when the melody of monsoon spills over,
and windswept darkness caresses her desires,
the rhythm of raindrops plays on her parched skin,
the fragrance of kadams carries the scent of her lover,
her wishes run amok,
she becomes a yearing Radha,
her body still pulsating like a string
after it has been played upon

She hears the familiar sound
of soft snoring by her side.
Lying wide wide awake; unsated
she looks out into the wet darkness of the night,
its deep dark gaze akin to her love.
Her heart croons,
Ami tomar preme hobo sabar kolonkobhagi
(*In your love I will embrace all the ignominies*)

The night knows her secret,
her tale of betrayal.

shravan or *srabon* (Bengali)– monsoon month
kadam– monsoon bloom
Ami tomar preme hobo sobar–a line from a Tagore song

Renewal

There is a sense of renewal
as the green thrusts itself from
the brown bark of the tree,
trusting the warmth of the sun.
I too, push open the window
the printed curtain,
the dusty writing desk,
the drawer full of inked love of long ago
melts in the gold of the sun.
I close my eyes
half truths cover half lies.
The sparrows are lovers like us, the morning after,
the window sill holds them as
they are all over each other.
I am left with the forgotten sensation of me flowing,
the boundaries of our skin merging...
rewriting new script
–the warmth of your mouth on mine.

The slice of the peeping sky becomes a sheet
my rippling desires scribbled on it
Will you check mail?
Will you drop in?

Remembrance

Someday you too
may forget me
in fact, we are all forgotten somewhere in time.
Like the long dark shadows of night are forgotten
by sunbathed verandahs,
with queued up pickle jars,
delightfully basking in golden rays.

Still, I shall remain like an ancient relic,
carved desire in stone,
standing still; waiting
on moon blanched nights
with patience of a hermit.
Meanwhile, flowers will bloom
and at times you might look at
the melting melancholy of the sunset sky and wonder,
what makes you feel so akin to it?

And someday, on a lonely trail of a misty dream,
you might feel me
and our deep desired kisses,
and realize,
that I am missing
since long.

Palette

Someday, somewhere in time,
love becomes a lone goldfish, its mouth agape
breathing out emptiness
that slowly seeps into the palette of my eyes
spilling over
to the roads and markets and buildings,
bustling yet lonely,
I write verses for the city.

The words are like plankton; floating,
drifting ,in the muddy water
of remembrance.

There are rows of halogen lamps,
faraway on the bridge
their luminance swims in the river
river that carries the tales of my eyes
eyes that cradle dreams
dreams that drape blue
blue that is lonesome
oozing out as ink,
I write verses for you.

July Rains

After the rains
I kiss your cappuccino mouth,
tongues circling, searching eternity,
filling the deep spaciousness with an urgency.
An envelope of rapid breaths
makes us look like the sunset sky,
smudged amber and vermilion,
relic of love and lush forest of desire on our skin
inhaling the musk of the wet wet earth.

After the cappuccino years
I fall in love with the other things,
green tea, yoga, photography
and forget how it feels to have
the rush of distilled starlight within.
With time, we grow to become islands,
there are no dates to remember either,
only the tongue has a saved memory
where a wee bit of July still lingers.

When You Return

It might be a summer day
when you return.
The red of the April sun spreading,
the cotton dreams drying on the clothesline,
a book of forbidden love;
resting upturned on the bosom–
a thirst to take sip of the fleeting bubbling youth.
Life passing by the narrow lane on a lonely languid noon

A wait lulls–
the open beak of the crow,
the wafting smell of ripening mangoes.
There's a wait too in the parched skin of the green,
there's a wait, as the sky slowly darkens.

The night hears the drumming sound of the rains,
a fragile corner of the heart quivers,
a fairy tale longs to reach its end.

Another Day

It is just another day,
my listerine washed mouth;
the laundry waiting in soap filled tub
the routine of bread, jam and coffee
and moving away from fragile dreams of the night.

It is just another day,
pedestrians on city pavements;
the afternoon sun's spillage on giant billboards,
burp of dosa sambar at Udipi restaurant
and the crammed metro ride back to the known shadows.

It is just another day,
I wish to kick the routine
spread my skin against the warmth of yours,
time is fluid; I swim across it,
my ripening lust a cartographer;
shortening the tyranny of distance
words become sound spinning in the air,
the mole on your chin trembles in my glass,
the strawberry of your bubblegum mouth
wrap around my tongue.

The frustration of a lonely bed is a python.
I die. I die to become a wish weaving stories in your eyes
till the tingling of the wind
chime becomes the clamour of a beginning.
Another day.

Rainy Days

It's always the rain that does the trick,
bringing us back,
through almost forgotten lanes,
like the trailing tune of Chaurasia's flute.

I look at you; somewhat in a daze
you look so young; fresh from college
green hearts spinning like mad windmills
green hopes spread all over Maidan

Through the acres of green we rush
till its abundance wanes to dull grey
tufts of dried wilted grass; losing its way
to the soot and dust of today.

Yet some days are like the homing birds
returning to my eyes in all their verdant hues,
dripping down my sooty window pane
reminiscent of a youthful me and you.

Green

Life and its accumulated filth
clog the arteries.
The tubes and monitors
hear the wheeze.
Memories are like flashing meteors,
and just before sinking into the dark,
a desire leaps up like an eager frog
from the fluid of the bile
–rain drenched leaves and fields,
an endless stretch,
and a run across the wet wet green.

Summer

The dry scalp of the earth
parched cowdung cakes on mud walls,
the smoky *chullah*,
spluttering sound of mustard,
wafting smell of raw mangoes,
–a baby swings
the mother hums a rain song
while looking up
at the blazing *chaitra* sky.

Chullah– mud oven
Chaitra– name of a summer month in Bengali

When Love Becomes a Four Letter Word

The large bay window opens out to the sea. A mellow morning has unfolded, I look at the silvery spread of the sand and beyond that, the blue of the ocean; sparkling occasionally.

I dip a tea bag in my cup, letting the infusion drown the unquiet mornings I left behind, mornings that were marked by several voices, *Ananda Bazar Patrika*, cups of milky hot tea accompanied by Britannia biscuits and few quivering moments of sindur (vermillion) smudged togetherness with you. Those have long since receded like waves.

Time is like a mystic saint, transforms itself to a tiny hyphen between now and then. A kaleidoscope of frames rush towards me along with the brine of the sea. The bird songs of spring, the melancholy of autumn leaves converge seamlessly. I become the sea wind; laden with the saltiness of all that has happened The fading moments slow dance in my eyes, our old lane broadens to a dazzling beach where I stand alone amidst empty sea shells. I call out your name. There is no audible sound, only a trembling of the air and an after taste of milky frothy days.

Honeysuckle

It's the morning after, I stand alone against the vast glass window overlooking a city that is yawning out of sleep. Droplets of the night still linger on me.

I wear the sky; its pale blue stretches on my skin,our secret drips from my jojoba scented hair; my face, my neck, my arms, soft and supple in the mist of lavender still gleam with the remains of an unworded poem. The redness of your impatience blush faintly on my skin, I smile.

My longing is like the deep deep furrow that cuts the sky, perhaps taking you back to your city by the sea.

My eyelashes become a painter's brush; they paint the previous night in amorous colours.

A honeysuckle plant embraces me along the path of your fingers and drunk in its scent, the borders of our skin merge to become a sea, the silvery rays of the night sky waltz to the lilt and rush of our waves.

Time is just a mole on my chin that you miss.

Your red heart flutters and flies in like a buzzing bee I see petals unfurling slowly.

I grow radiant with the blooming flowers.

Monologue

The asphalt on my city's street knows me well.
The blazing yellow of the cabs,
the tea stalls,
the strong roots of the trees forcing
their way up the sidewalks,
have heard my footsteps.

A breezy summer noon
and an unruly scarf is swept across my neck
Its bold hues and dense kalamkari curves
reminds me of my grandma's bed– four poster, ornate.
I used to listen to her tales with rapt attention.
I have always been a good listener and she;
a story teller, betel juice stuck at her mouth's corner.

You say, time is a concept.
To me, it is often a long winding road,
its turns and bends bringing in another season,
the puddles of joy, chai and pakoras, drenched emotions.
My eyes are travellers without maps,
treading on landscapes with the rhythm of rain
pouring over the Hooghly river,
the collage of country boats and a longing to
smudge all the known colours.

A white envelope arrives and sends me
packing my bags for Bhagalpur .

The train chugs out leaving behind a chaotic station,
the city; my muse.
and I suddenly realize why autumn comes
wrapped in melancholic hues

chai– tea
pakora– fritters
Kalamkari–a particular weave

Life Events

The chiffon night is a marquee
It's well past seven and
I look out of my hotel window to see a hilly town below,
dotted with glowworm lights.
Time is like a blob of butter in my soup bowl,
melting, and I see myself
walking along the trails of our scar.
The flow chart of our life events
are pages of different books we wish to
read and then wish away.
The silence of the hills makes me
crawl into myself, here it is quiet,
here you are mine.
A person is only a few digits away.
A strange oscillation– should I or should I not?
My heart hears sounds of fluttering wings while
the beep on my phone screen decides that
I need to return.
A heaviness hangs over.
Once again I make a choice to depart,
leaving behind the hills and us.

Routine

The monotony of the day drooped and merged
with the lonely shadow of the evening. The dimly
lit cafe at the other end of the road was the only
heartwarming sign to her as she took long strides
towards it, entered and with a regular ease, seated
herself at the corner seat and ordered her black
coffee and scones.
The day was done and a flock of weary faces was
heading back home.

The glass window offered her a slice of the grey
skyline. She looked on; nonchalant; emptying her
loneliness in small sips.
A mute door and four blue walls awaited the click
of her key.

The ritual of coffee and scones was over,
it was time to leave.
She lit a cigarette.

The smoke curled up and scattered like her shape-
less thoughts.

There was no paper or ink; she felt the wood of
the tabletop and how her finger had unfailingly
scribbled the letters of his name.

Bradshaw Villa

The mist curled up,
the tall shadows of pines stood still on
the window panes.
The smoky eyes of the night heaved a sigh.
The spectre of a young life stubbed out,
loomed large over the moor.
Moth-eaten memories;
stashed away in grandma's trunk stifled a yawn.
The pale blanketed moon,
the attic, the stairways, the lonely rooms
witnessed a death avenged.
At the crack of dawn,
the grey-haired keeper creaked open the villa's gate.
The mellow light of the
early sun announced his master's death.
Horror writ large on the time-ravaged face,
the buried stories their ensnared tentacles
had wrung out his last breath.
The cruel hand that shot his free willed wife;
hung helpless and cold

A silent teardrop, the master had lost his battle
with the phantom of the night.
A photo id card lying by,
sent a shiver down his spine
The past had come lapping on the shores of time

The young beaming face on the card
looked familiar to the one that remained
hung from the wall,
the smiling hazelnut eyes, a baby held in her arms.
The card read,

LISA BRADSHAW
Investigating Journalist

The locals confirmed seeing
the young lady climb up the moor,
she had said, she came in search of her roots.

Forgetting

Finally he left,
after years of lonely wandering
and the gradual fading away of faces
from the heart's hemline.
The blur thickened mind;
weary of travelling let the body sink.
The swaying shadows of neem leaves
on the window pane
saw him depart.

Breathless,
nude,
foamy froth
by the side of his mouth
where words remained stuck,
like some unwritten poems–
the crimson promises of his first love,
that lost its green
yet clung to him as a dull ache.

A gaped mouth– an escaped silence,
her pale smile, brimming eyes
bobbed up from a pool of blinding white,
Her name, eaten up by amnesia.

Beyond

On some days
when you've peeled the layers of remembrance
and I appear to be a faraway isle
that can only be reached through a digital click
you pause and weep; looking at our pix.
I tiptoe by your side;
run my fingers through your messy salt and pepper,
There are wishes that take the shape of clouds
Softly, I tell you, how to float beyond.

Yes, I have ticked away like the hands of a clock
a dropped moment,
curling up like mist
amidst the memory of rhododendrons,
or lying amidst chipped tales of sea shells
looking up at the lovely cerulean spread

Still, I will be there by your side,
when you have walked those long miles,
with zillions of calming rays rushing towards you
sucking you into the darkening bright mouth of
time's tunnel.
You will hear my voice
in each lub dub of your faint heartbeat,
as I call you by my name.

The Body Saga

The certainty of life was reached.
Each weary cell whispered to the other.

Life had been a crossword puzzle,
a constant search
Touches were saved memories,
good or bad.
The first flush of womanhood
in droplets of warm blood,
made the body blossom
The eyes became a path,
to the smell of rain and wet earth,
the rush of love branching all over,
a cocooned desire swam in the body's pool.

Years later, the sagging skin;
a washed shore after the waves recede,
a wrinkled wish tattooed on wrist,
the body was worn out, heavily heaved.

The world that was cupped in hand,
spilled and scattered,
the wheezing sound of betrayed breaths,
the accumulated pus of life spread to each cell,
till the warmth flowed out.

The news spread
in social networking sites,
the body was wished a peaceful rest.

Winter In Me

A winter resides in me
a morgue-ish cold,
no green grows; only a stark whiteness thrives.
Unaware of it,
I step aside from this mundane life to look back.
Rewind.

A kohl rimmed dusk looks plaintively
some nameless sorrows wander across the western sky,
they are the flakes of our lost selves
searching for the time left behind,
but our fatigued memories like
shut doors lead us nowhere,
the rehearsed words get muted
in the buzz of the busy cities
that lie between us
A distance gets blurred with an erasure of time
time ,through which the poet had travelled to *Natore*
to look into the eyes of his *Banalata Sen*,
an emptiness slithers through my veins,
something hard and icy has remained
stuck since long.
Is it the lost time?
–frozen?
–turned into winter?

Natore is a place in modern Bangladesh, used by renowned Bengali
poet, *Jibananda Das* in his remarkable poem, *Banalata Sen*

Sleep

The earth sings me a lullaby of how it drained my love,
sip by sip , while spinning tirelessly
and how you and I kept on moving;
like letters with wrong addresses not reaching anywhere.

Now I see you,
a faraway figure moving far and farther beyond our sky
that was once tinged with love's afterglow,
going somewhere beyond time,
time, that was all ours ,
we had measured it in moments
till it stretched to days, years, decades.

The shadows grew longer; you turned to a story
told, re told, and remembered through old photographs.
Now, a thousand years of sleep between us.

A Tale of Flesh

A fish gulped the ring of Shakuntala,
later it was discovered by a fisherman
–so goes the ancient lore of love reconciled.

A fish grows fertile like a woman
drinking the tales of love; of life.

A silvery desire,
auspiciously sent in the trousseau; with bridal finery,
lives and customs encircling its body,
later, each succulent part relished,
the leftover bones chewed to dust
by the cat of the house, licking paws; satiated.

For many, here in Bengal, fish is a way of life
For some women suddenly gone missing,
it is a way to get consumed likewise,
their flesh etched in charcoal; breathe as wall graffiti
the nonchalant Kolkata traffic speeds on.

The ancient lore reversed.

Escape

The mind's eye is a white washed wall
a void flutters its wings,
memories recycled, reused,
labyrinth of twisted congested streets;
have left a vacuum, the size of a continent.

It is only the monstrous 'now'
and faded the floral patterns of my heart
on a late night drive along the EM Bypass.
The vigilant lights stand still.
I pass by *Tara singh ka dhaba*,
the cool confines of my car
resist the familiar favourite aroma of
tandoori and tadka... and endless talk...
and endless us.

The wheels tear apart the night
I gulp down the liquid darkness around me
The past is relentless,
its glaring eyes come looking for me.
Are they bringing back the memories?
I try to swerve and escape
a flood of warmth gushes out,
the drowning of voices,
colours emptying the eyes,
then all is quiet.
White.

Scattered

An ice cube in my glass is a silent room,
its walls slowly melting,
spreading a cool numbness
across the fluid night.
I take a sip.
I flow through the night.

An old lane walks out of my eyes,
narrow
forsaken,
my limbs flow through it;
it then widens and widens
to become a river,
eager to touch you.

Sleep and only sleep makes you a possibility,
an undefined vagueness of my conflicts and loss.
I see a torn turquoise string; its blueness scattered,
I sit up, trying to figure out if it is the colour of pain.

Sunset Hues

My window overlooks a slice of our lane
by the corner stands a gulmohor;
bursting in flames
My weary eyes take a sip of the scarlet,
scarlet; as it has slowly ebbed,
the dry months,
the empty nest
Like me, my beloved porcelains
wait behind the glass case
they are hardly in use these days.
The framed moments keep smiling at me,
they are wiped clean by my old maid

Time keeps crawling on my wrist,
as it turns five;
I slip into my walking shoes
and walk out of the apartment.
I step on the velvety green of the park,
here I have some like minded friends.
I walk as briskly as I can while looking out for them.
A splurge of colours makes me stop in my track,
the sky is smeared in sunset hues;
red, amber, purple.
Awed by this magnificence, I take a deep breath,
I fall in love with the afterglow
I fall in love with life that has gone slow.

Trapped

My CT scan report says my lungs are vessels,
my brimming heartache, fostered happiness.
I strain my eyes to focus and see
few things floating in the cystic fluid,
with skin and bones, cells and membranes
they have grown to become me.

The innocence of broken crayons,
one turquoise earring,
the other of the pair lost in lovemaking
a blue pottery salad bowl, our honeymoon souvenir,
my chipped china cup, morning ritual of tea.
the bright luminosity of their half
drowned tales bobbing in the slimy
green of moth eaten memory.

My breath is a trapped bird, fluttering wings,
the wheezing sound doodles the shape of desire
in the air of the room,
blotted outline of an unread memoir,
a tiresome wait tries to reach your lips,
the urgency of life gets caught in a grey chaos, gasps,
my lungs shrink to look like a stubbed out cigarette butt.
The fluid spills.

Epilogue

An evening is a fading line
stretched towards the tenderness of home,
the remains of the day spread
as hues of remembrance
my grandma's patient finger passing through
each rosary bead;
life's countless memories.
we carry such an evening within us,
often unaware,
like crows sitting in a row till
the fall of darkness of the shadows.

The smudged kohl line of a broken promise
unnoticed in the mad rush of a city;
its tired and crumbling walls
the roads and parks and boulevards
melting into a strange soundlessness,
the muddy river water washes
the betrayals of the body; the wreckage of life.
A name gathers the grey of the dusk,
an evening is the closure of a book,
a pain of parting;
the last line of an epilogue.

MALLIKA BHAUMIK

Mallika Bhaumik has a Master's degree in English literature from the University of Calcutta. She is passionate about reading and writing. She has been widely published both in India and abroad. Her first book of poems, *Echoes*, has won the *Reuel International Award* for the best debut poetry collection in 2018. She lives and writes from Kolkata.

www.ingramcontent.com/pod-product-compliance
Lightning Source LLC
Chambersburg PA
CBHW032052040426
42449CB00007B/1085